The History of Money

By Linda Crotta Brennan

Illustrated by Rowan Barnes-Murphy

The Child's World®

Published by The Child's World®
1980 Lookout Drive • Mankato, MN 56003-1705
800-599-READ • www.childsworld.com

Acknowledgments
The Child's World®: Mary Berendes, Publishing Director
The Design Lab: Design and production
Red Line Editorial: Editorial direction

Design elements: Eric Krouse/Dreamstime

ISBN 9781614732457
LCCN 2012932823

Printed in the United States of America
Mankato, MN
July 2012
PA02122

About the Author

Linda Crotta Brennan has a master's degree in early childhood education. She has taught elementary school and worked in a library. Now, she is a full-time writer. She enjoys learning new things and writing about them. She lives with her husband and goofy golden retriever in Rhode Island. She has three grown daughters.

About the Illustrator

Rowan Barnes-Murphy has created images and characters for children's and adults' books. His drawings have appeared in magazines and newspapers all over the world. He's even drawn for greeting cards and board games. He lives and works in Dorset, in southwest England, and spends time in rural France, where he works in an ancient farmhouse.

Jack skidded to a stop in front of Mia and Tomás's lemonade stand. "Boy, am I thirsty!" He emptied his pockets. "I don't have any money. I just have this shell I found at the beach."

Mia picked it up. "It's pretty. May I have it for my collection?"

"Sure," said Jack. "It's a trade!"

Uncle Tito had stopped by the lemonade stand to see how sales were going. "You two are **bartering**, the oldest way of doing business," he said.

Tomás poured Jack some lemonade. "We talked about bartering in school with Miss Singh," he said. "Long ago, weren't shells used for money?"

"They were," Uncle Tito said. "People in China and Africa used cowrie shells as money. Native Americans used beads made out of clamshells. The beads are called **wampum**."

"My mom has a wampum necklace," said Mia. "Hey, look who's here! It's Miss Singh!"

"Hi, kids!" said Miss Singh. "I was out for a walk and saw your stand. Did I hear you talking about money?"

"Yes!" exclaimed Mia. "Jack paid for his lemonade with a shell, and we started talking about bartering."

"And money," add Tomás.

"I see," Miss Singh replied. "People have used all sorts of things as money: cows, grain, beads, fur, chocolate . . ."

"Chocolate money!" shouted Jack. "That sounds delicious."

Everyone laughed.

Money can be anything that a group of people values and accepts for trade. Imagine something you and your friends might use for money.

"When did people start using real money?" asked Tomás.

"Do you mean money like this?" said Uncle Tito, pulling coins and bills out of his pocket. He paid Tomás for a cup of lemonade. "First, they used metals such as gold and silver."

"People would carry rings or chunks of silver and gold," added Miss Singh. "Or they would use jewelry to buy things. Businesses would weigh the metal."

"The first real coins were made many, many centuries ago," Miss Singh continued. "They were a mixture of gold and silver called **electrum**. They were easy to carry. They didn't need to be weighed."

"More and more countries started to use coins," added Uncle Tito.

"People in China started to use spade- and knife-shaped coins," Miss Singh said. "Eventually, they switched to coins that were more round that had a hole in the middle. The hole made it possible to carry these coins on strings."

"Depending on what metal was available," said Uncle Tito, "coins were made of bronze, copper, gold, or silver. At first, only wealthy people used coins. Most people still bartered for everyday items."

"Using money was easier than bartering," added Miss Singh. "You could buy all sorts of goods and services with money. You could use it to figure out how much something was worth. And since money didn't rot or go bad, you could store your wealth."

The first known coins were created almost 3,000 years ago. They were made in a country called Lydia in what is now Turkey. Soon, the use of coins spread to other areas, including Greece and India.

"What about paper money?" asked Jack. "That's even lighter than coins."

"China is the first country known to use paper money," explained Miss Singh. "Hundreds of years went by before paper money was used in Europe. That didn't happen until the 1600s."

"What about in America?" asked Tomás.

"Early colonists used a mixture of money," said Uncle Tito. "They used Indian wampum, furs, tobacco, and French, English, and Spanish coins."

"Each colony in America issued its own money, too," added Miss Singh. "It could be very confusing."

The Spanish real was a popular coin. People would split it into eight bits, or pieces, to make change. Two bits were one-fourth—a quarter—of a real (2/8 = 1/4). Two bits became a term for the US quarter and 25¢. Some people still refer to a quarter or 25¢ as two bits.

"When did we get regular US money?" asked Jack.

"In the late 1700s, after the United States officially became a nation," said Uncle Tito. "The government created the US **Mint** in 1792. It mints, or makes, US coins. The first coins were copper cents. Soon, the mint was making gold and silver coins, too."

The US Mint estimates that a US coin will last **25** years.

"What about paper money in the United States?" asked Mia.

"Coins became scarce in the 1860s, during the Civil War. People were afraid. Many **hoarded** their gold and silver coins. And other metals were needed for the war," explained Miss Singh. "Also, wars are expensive. The government needed money to pay for the war."

"So, the government made paper money?" Tomás asked.

"Yes," Miss Singh replied. "But people didn't have much trust in paper money."

"But it was from the government," replied Mia. "Oh, wait, I think I know. Was it because people weren't used to using paper money?"

"Exactly," said Uncle Tito, pulling a dollar bill out of his pocket. "Today, the US Bureau of Engraving and Printing prints paper money in five cities. Its locations in Washington DC and Fort Worth, Texas, have tours and you can see money being printed," he said.

"I'd like to see that," said Tomás. "Maybe they'd give us a sample, like when we went to the candy factory and saw how it was made."

Uncle Tito chuckled. "Chocolate isn't like money anymore!"

When someone uses a **bank card**, the bank's computer keeps track of how much money they spend electronically from their account.

"Hmm," Jack hummed, scratching his head. "Usually, my parents don't use paper dollars or coins. They use a bank card to buy things."

"I know what you mean," Uncle Tito responded, opening his wallet. "Credit cards, debit cards, gas cards. I have more plastic than money."

"Money is always changing," said Miss Singh. "We went from bartering to using metals, then to using coins, and then to using paper money. Now, we buy things with bank cards. Electronic money is the new money revolution."

"Imagine what money will be like when we're grown up," said Tomás.

Mia grinned. "I can't wait to find out."

Glossary

bank card (BANGK kahrd): A bank card is a small, rectangular piece of plastic given to you by a bank to buy items. If it is a debit card, the money will come directly from your bank account. If it is a credit card, you will owe the bank the money you spend. Jack's parents use bank cards to buy things.

barter (BAHR-tur): To swap goods or services without using money is to barter. Mia bartered her lemonade for Jack's shell.

electrum (i-LEK-truhm): Electrum is a mixture of gold and silver. The first coins were made of electrum.

hoard (hord): When you hoard something, you keep and store it. During the Civil War, Americans hoarded their gold and silver coins.

mint (mint): To make coins is to mint them. A mint is also the place where coins are made. The United States mints several coins, including nickels and pennies.

wampum (WAHM-puhm): Wampum is beads made from shells and strung together to make items such as necklaces and belts. Some Native Americans used wampum as money. The colonist gave the Native American wampum for some corn.

Books

Adler, David A. *Money Madness*. New York: Holiday House, 2009.

Rau, Dana Meachen. *The History of Money*. Milwaukee: Weekly Reader Early Learning Library, 2006.

Somervill, Barbara A. *The History of Money*. Chanhassen, MN: Child's World, 2006.

Web Sites

Visit our Web site for links about the history of money:
childsworld.com/links

Note to Parents, Teachers, and Librarians: We routinely verify our Web links to make sure they are safe and active sites. So encourage your readers to check them out!

Index